Well, I've now spent more years in Bristol, England than I have anywhere else as an adult. That's more than six years by the time you've read this. And though not many British folk would agree, I've lost a lot of that Kentucky accent; folks back home do look at me funny, ask me where I'm from. I am from Kentucky but do feel like I'm from a lot of different places spread out all over the world by now. Though my backpacking, living abroad days are mostly behind me, I've been fortunate to do some travelling these last couple of years though only for a week or two at a time as opposed to the months of freewheeling I was used to from my 20s. I feel the pull of Kentucky/Tennessee home now more than I ever have. I reckon that comes from having my own family and realizing how important family is. I've my own little boy now who you'll meet in these poems. I'd say you'll also meet, briefly, some of the more inner journeys I've been on as I gain a little age, thinking all the way back to my own childhood, farther back than my memory will go even. Being a family man now, my writing has necessarily changed as the times I have to write tend to come in big chunks when I can get a day or half day to myself and then all that writing that needs to come out comes out. And here's some of that regurgitation here for you. This bio can only give so much of my life; you can get a little bit more from these here poems.

From Tennessee, into fatherhood, high on a mountain trail, along the river, and through everyday occurrences, ¿Who Knows? reports back on what's happening, what's been seen, what's been felt, all from one particular, peculiar, point of view. These poems were written in brief moments, strung together to provide a thread through parts of my life; a point of view, a philosophy of life, whatever you want to call it, mine shows here, hinted at, pointed to, inherent in the very process of writing and found under the stones of the words laid down. I've put a lot of time into mostly Tang Dynasty and earlier Chinese poetry(unfortunately, in translation) which served to inform western poetry's modernist movement which led to the Beats who in turn led me to that Chinese source material in the first place.

There's a lot of place happening in these particular poems; more poems about my home and family in Kentucky. Despite living for more than five years in South Korea, it wasn't until a recent visit that I actually wrote about my favorite place in Korea, Bukhansan. Two of my favorite places in England get featured in quite a few poems: Frog Mill where the Buddhafield Village Retreat is held each year, and a certain part of the Frome Valley Walkway where it comes into Bristol.

Poetry for me has always been about making a record of moments in my life, as long as those moments see me with my notebook to hand. These moments can capture a feeling or simply record an event; at the best of times I suppose the poems manage to convey the scene or the feeling of a moment. If you read this, then read these poems, I hope some of my transport comes across to you and, most of all, I hope you enjoy the poems, whatever they may do for you.

Jeremy Toombs
January 2017

¿Who Knows?

Jeremy Toombs

Burning Eye

BurningEyeBooks
Never Knowingly
Mainstream

Copyright © 2017 Jeremy Toombs

The author asserts the moral right under the Copyright, Designs and Patents Act 1988 to be identified as the author of this work.

All rights reserved. No part of this publication may be reproduced, stored in a retrieval system, or transmitted, in any form or by any means without the prior written consent of the author, nor be otherwise circulated in any form of binding or cover other than that in which it is published and without a similar condition being imposed on the subsequent purchaser.

This edition published by Burning Eye Books 2017

www.burningeye.co.uk

@burningeyebooks

Burning Eye Books
15 West Hill, Portishead, BS20 6LG

ISBN 978 1 90913 697 7

¿Who Knows?

CONTENTS

FRIDAY, MAY 27TH, 7:14 AM GMT	10
NORTH FROM ATLANTA	11
MAY 29TH, PORT ROYAL PARK THUNDERSTORM / SPRING SOFT RAIN FALLS	12
	13
CARRY ON	14
KUDZU	15
LEAVING TENNESSEE	16
LEFT BEHIND	17
DETROIT AIRPORT	18
SOME SAY SOME DAYS ARE HARDER	19
BENJAMIN	20
ON HAVING A LITTLE BABY	21
BABY CHILD GOING FOR THE TEAT SAYS	22
BENJAMIN! WHAT?	23
EARLY SUMMER'S AFTERNOON	24
THAT LITTLE BOY	25
STREAMSIDE PICNIC WITH THAT LITTLE BOY	26
LITTLE MOUNTAIN BOY	27
BELLY WELL	28
FIRST MISSION: GET TO THE MOUNTAIN	29
IF WE HAD BEEN / EARTHWORMS	30
BUKHANSAN	31
TWO AND A HALF	32
BURNT	33

LOOKING BEYOND	34
VIEWING THE MOON TEMPLE	35
KOREAN COURTYARD	
IMMORTAL MAGNOLIA	36
FRIDAY, APRIL 1ST, 4:15 PM KST	37
GETTING CLOSE	38
DUST	39
OFF MOUNTAIN, ON ROAD	40
KOREAN NIGHT RAIN	41
FROME RIVER VALLEY WALK	42
LITTLE OTTER	43
EASTVILLE PARK	44
SOME PICTURES	45
FROG MILL	46
DRINKING WINE WITH WESTRAY AFTER NOT SEEING HIM FOR A LONG TIME	48
CREME EGG	49
MISSION BURRITO	50
THURSDAY NIGHT	51
IN THE DESERT WITH JESUS	52
IT NEVER LEAVES ME	53
ON THE TV AT CASA CURVO	54
HOW I CAUGHT A FALLING BOTTLE	55
LITTLE BABY JEREMY	56
CHINA EXHIBIT, BRITISH MUSEUM	57
FREEDOM	58
¿WHO KNOWS?	59

FRIDAY, MAY 27TH, 7:14 AM GMT

Early morning goodbye:
       so sweet that boy,
              so perfect my wife.
I'm off to Nashville:
city bus to airport bus
       to airport plane,
              KLM Flight #1050.
East to Amsterdam.
West then to Hotlanta.
North to Nashville.
       My father, my brother, my nephews
picking me up
eighteen hours from now.
Listening to Willie, to Merle.
Talking to my wife and my boy
just before boarding.
A sigh
on the way to the gate
leaves me no better off.

Oh, just a wee little
bottle of wine colored red
gone straight to me head.
Feelin' fine now,
going down into Amsterdam.

NORTH FROM ATLANTA

Looking out the window: Tennessee.
Nashville coming up.
I never have found suitable words for this feeling: coming home.
Past times linger longer here,
transcend my wanderings, my years,
waiting for me even
up here at 10,000 feet,
bumping through the clouds
covering those central Tennessee rolling hills.
Getting on to night time.
A big ol' lake down below,
the water fitting just so to the shore.

MAY 29TH, PORT ROYAL PARK

Flooded Red River running fast;
water's gone down nine, maybe ten feet.
I can see on the other shore
grasses water-combed over pointing downstream,
mud bank caved in,
flotsam running by.
I've known this river
most my life and though it flows
minute to minute through the same rust-red mud
it ain't never minute to minute been the same.

THUNDERSTORM /
SPRING SOFT RAIN FALLS

Lightning brightens the night for a moment.
The imprint on mind lasts longer.
Thunder rolls around the sky.
Thunder rolls around the sky.
Rain keeps falling.
My folks are sleeping unless the rainfall on the roof,
the thunder or the lightning woke them.
Lightning gets brighter.
Thunder gets louder.
Rain falls harder, shakes the leaves.
I hear a roar off northeast of here. Sounds like a train.
Like a train horn blowing, like a train rumbling.
Train or wind, it's moving down now, away.
Rain, thunder, lightning moving on, away.
Rain falls gentle now.
There's a smell in the air: I can't tell you about it.
Crickets singing now.
What else can be said
about a regular old spring storm?

CARRY ON

The land in form of fields: corn, wheat, tobacco, soybeans.
With a sigh I know I'm not likely to live here.
Middle-aged now, nearly, for the first time
I feel the pull of home.
Home in the early summer heat, trees, old stories and ruminations.

I've been gone now so long from home.
What could I do now
but carry on?

KUDZU

All over roadside trees, power lines,
the dark green vines
rearing up down back roads like
      an elephant, a dinosaur,
alive, present.

It's this that I am,
what all of us are: alive,
present in any form, like kudzu.

> Kudzu was introduced into the southeast United States from East Asia. It was promoted as cattle fodder, a cover plant to stop erosion, and even as an ornamental plant. But kudzu took over to the point it was put on the noxious weed list. Those vines are still around, though, and growing.

LEAVING TENNESSEE

The tarmac looks like a still lake.
Rain's incessant.
Looking out these windows,
tuned in to Billy Joe Shaver,
leaving Tennessee again.

LEFT BEHIND

Something's left behind: thoughts of my brother,
how I'm glad to see him off,
how he leaves me tense, irritable.
It's better off if I just don't say nothing.
Words could bring the fight part of me wants; I've seen it.
But this fantasy is useless, nothing good to come of it.
I know from experience.

I'd rather he was just a normal guy.
I'd rather what he says wasn't all a lie.
I'd rather there's a god up there in the sky.
I'd rather he'd answered those old prayers by and by.
But he ain't there, never has been.
My brother don't care. Never has been
what he's said he is.
Me? My anger is old, cold, hard, and long stored away.
There's nothing at all
I can do about any of it.

DETROIT AIRPORT

The last meal: chicken, a biscuit, and mashed potatoes.
That's it, to quicken the blood.
There are those that don't understand
how a Kentucky man needs chicken in hand,
hand to mouth, mouth to belly
while I watch a bit of softball on the airport telly.
A leisurely lunch, not watching the time.
Jeremy Toombs, please report to the gate.
Oh, my, I'm running late. To the gate:
everybody's on board.
They're waiting on me and two other folks.
Fifteen minutes to take-off,
on the plane now and ready to go!

SOME SAY SOME DAYS ARE HARDER

I say a day is a day,
busy or still.
        Between sunrises
do ten thousand things.
Do nothing.
Do sit.
All the same.
Bit of shit.
Bit of shine.
Hang the washing on the line.
Willie playing "Blue Eyes."

I sleep well for being tired.
I wake well for having slept.

A tooth hurts.
Sun slips down the street
        through autumn leaves.

BENJAMIN

You are baby beginner's mind.
Stop now.
Ah, it's too late:
on the wheel,
on the teat.
All life is suffering.
At least we're in it together.

ON HAVING A LITTLE BABY

Having a little baby
is not so strange.
Mind shifts.
Heart fills.
This is normal
        now.
Wake feed sleep.
No problem.

BABY CHILD GOING FOR THE TEAT SAYS

We're animals.
Once was a day all of us
made the same move:
 feed feed,
sleep, feed again.
If my food was still free?
Why, that would be me again:
feed feed sleep feed again.

BENJAMIN! WHAT?

You don't know nothing.
Milk jug in your face
and you cry for milk.
What?

Today, we went to Wales,
another country, and you didn't even know.

What is this? What is it?
No words to know.
How to think?
You can't even see a foot away!
So what are you looking at?
I say Benji: you don't know nothing.

EARLY SUMMER'S AFTERNOON

Shakespeare's Holy Trinity Church
steeple just peaks over the trees.
The man himself buried inside
who has my birthday.

      Here we sit, Benji and me.
Midsummer Night's Dream
plays in the park for free.

Benji sits, watches,
rice cake in one hand,
rattle in the other, Shakespeare
going in his brain.

THAT LITTLE BOY

Big and little are not so far apart.
From where I sit I see both.
Good and bad don't really exist.
From where I sit things just are.

That little boy
is climbing on a table
made to look like roads, mountains, a lake.
How big that little boy is
to the table people, their cars turned over.

Is this good? For the table people: surely a catastrophe!
Freak of nature! Such a giant playing with table people's cars like
    toys!

Is this good? Is this bad?
Just ask the table people.
They don't say nothing.

STREAMSIDE PICNIC WITH THAT LITTLE BOY

Wind blowing gentle.
Sun shining softly.
Chipmunk on a bough.
Chipmunk jumps
rock to rock,
climbs trees up and down.
Where'd he go?
Who knows?

Oh, look, to his tree again,
back to the water.
Where'd he go again?
What happened?
On his tree again
and down to the water.
Look!

LITTLE MOUNTAIN BOY

Up in the mountains with that little boy,
Benny Bunny's smile lasts for a while.
Throwing sticks on rocks, leaves in the air,
laughing at this world
up in the mountains with that little boy.

River rock stepping means
watch your feet rock to rock.
Jump over the pools
full of tadpoles.
Sun shines on this boy of mine
up in the mountains with that little boy.

Blue Bukhansan bandanna blanket,
kimbap, banana, mountain stream picnic,
up in the mountains with that little boy.

BELLY WELL

Spread out over a mountain hike
three *kimbap* rolls
still fill the belly well.

FIRST MISSION: GET TO THE MOUNTAIN

Underground hike subway transfer:
airport line to line number one is done.
Must've taken ten, fifteen minutes.

Now I can see the hills,
the mountains, out the train window,
the train having moved
above ground.

Aye, this is the day's theme: Movin' On Up!

IF WE HAD BEEN / EARTHWORMS

If we had been
Buddhist monks
in a past life
we wouldn't have been
very good monks.

It would mean more,
be better now,
had we been earthworms.

BUKHANSAN

Mountain creek flow
        down on the right,
Sapaesan rises above to the north,
mountain access road ends soon,
magpie flies off.

Pine trees, bare branches, blossoms,
some spring green showing through.

Everywhere is home.
Body is home.
Mind is home.
Here we go now: Bukhansan home.

TWO AND A HALF

Two and a half kilometres
to the Hoeryong mountain crossroads.

North towards Sapaesan
along Sapae ridgeline.

Eat most of a *chamchi kimbap*, a choco pie,
write
sit
go.

Sapaesan: a view east to Uijeongbu, south to Dobongsan.
What can be said
on top of a mountain?

Look!

I want my wife here,
my son.
He's too small yet, too young to climb.
So they're in town
shopping.

The mountain is saying
there is no loneliness
as it stands
or after it's gone.

How could all this be gone?
Just like you and me one day.
Just gone.

Crow on a bough on a mountain
looked at me and said, "Aack, aack,"
looked around, flew off.
That's pretty much all
any of us do.

BURNT

Somebody, something, some happening
has done burnt the west side of Podae ridgeline.
Underbrush gone, just black
all the way down, forty, fifty, a hundred yards
as far as sight can see.

Charcoal smell of burnt trees
wafts about on the breeze with some still standing.

The fire helicopter flies circles around the mountain
dumping water
all day long.

LOOKING BEYOND

Looking beyond Wondobong Valley
from Mangwolsa
I see
Big Belly Buddha Rock Monk
just sitting there
looking north.

VIEWING THE MOON TEMPLE

A visit to Mangwolsa.

There are times for viewing
the moon, in late afternoon.

I'm leaving Mangwolsa
as the sun slips behind
mountain ridge pines.

Mind and heart and mountain
in concert beyond, beyond.

Beyond the ten thousand rocks
I'm going down
rock step to
 rock step.

KOREAN COURTYARD
IMMORTAL MAGNOLIA

Shorn of branches,
bare of leaves,
most limbs lopped off.

Mostly trunk, just stood there,
three stories tall.

Bare branches with white
magnolia blooms: conspicuous, large, bright, perfect.

FRIDAY, APRIL 1ST, 4:15 PM KST

Sun just over the trees
       started my ascent.
Sun just over the trees
       saw me start back down.

Sun slipping down west,
me slipping down east
on down this mountainside.
The Heart Sutra
floating through my head.

GETTING CLOSE

You think you're getting close
to being down off the mountain:
      steady dropping
         rock step to rock step.
Next to the creek's falling flow
      little mountain pools form.

Looking up, see yonder:
      through the valley,
        the city.
It's surprising to your mind you're still taller than a high-rise.
Well, that's what you get for thinking
you're almost down the mountain.

DUST

Bukhansan dust,
        particulate mountain matter
on my boots,
in my lungs,
and mountain water in my belly.

OFF MOUNTAIN, ON ROAD

In a shabby little restaurant
drinking *maekju*,
thinking of how Leo said
his father's first part of a session
would be one long pull
until most of the glass was empty,
just like I've just done.

Well, I've come down that mountain
as fast as I could.
Everything hurting but still I feel good.
Now I'm just sitting, just drinking a beer,
wishing I had me
just one good friend here.

KOREAN NIGHT RAIN

What grows from a memory?
From all this together, these days,
those days, this rain,
the waning heat of the day: all soaked in
through the skin, carried around in our heads
around neurons flashing like lightning.

A feeling, or the shadow of one known in the mind.
How do I feel?
Korean night rain asks and answers
never having to say a word.

FROME RIVER VALLEY WALK

Frome River, River Frome
running fast.
A flash of blue flies through,
kingfisher showing out for you.

Autumn day Frome walk,
bit of wet, bit of mud.
Wet rock seat, cliff overhang
where I hang, Frome Valley flow of river,
flow of rock.

Every now and then I stop.
Look to hillside bluff-top leaves.
Leaves of red, yellow.
Leaves of brown, some still green.

Some water drips drops
on rock, on leaves.
Frome Valley drop by drop
keeps moving on,
rock to rock to leaves,
Frome Valley breathes: *Let's keep moving on.*

Rocks overhang.
Leaves beneath wet.
Green lichen flows down.
River water below sounds off.

Tree roots, branch size,
reach over,
fly down through cracked rocks,
slide down through ground.
Ever-so-slow slide rooting
seeking reaching above around.

Here's big rock my home.
Frome Valley river flow.
Below here rocks grow
immeasurably slow.
These big walls in big rock home.
Frome Valley river flow
keeps moving on.

LITTLE OTTER

Little otter, little otter
playing on the bank!
Little otter, I'd like to know what you think
about the cold water, water so fast
where you dive and then swim and then come up at last.
Where do you live, little otter?
Come across and let's play! Come down the Frome River walkway
       with me today.

Little otter, little otter: he's disappeared
under the water.

EASTVILLE PARK

Sunday spring sun shines
down through the trees;
sun moves down through
foliage gap, hits me in the head.

Sun sets towards town.
Rush of traffic
rustle of leaves
red sun behind a cloud
under the maple tree
fallen leaves
leaves falling:
the fall coming in nice.

Leaving Frome Valley walk
to Eastville Park sunset:
how the light sets on the green.
There's something else
empty, easy
running through fall Frome Valley walk
to Eastville Park sunset.

SOME PICTURES

Sunday St. Andrew's sunshine.
Sitting, drinking wine, talking.
Balancing on logs,
finding secret paths.

Ashley Street Park sunshine, Monday afternoon,
willow blossoms fall in my lap, on my notebook.
For some reason,
I brush them off.

Late spring evening rain,
the bamboo peaks just past
the corner of the house.
Bright green leaves stand out.

It's a moody Monday
      early afternoon
in May Park woods.
I'm just walking around
looking at the trees.

Springtime sunshine,
wind blows cold yet.
   My mind wanders,
      blows around,
settling everywhere.

FROG MILL

Sunset, moonrise
on a purple moor.
Sheep off to the south.
Masses of clouds float by
on northwest wind.

At the top of Frog Mill: eight-hundred-year-old mill ruins,
Devapriya's stupa looking over it all.

*

Waxing moon
        near to half full
up half way
        in a light blue sky.
What are we doing here?
Just waiting around, looking at the clouds.

*

Two blue jet aeroplanes
        southeast to northwest
          and vice versa:
low low low: just above the moor
so so so fast sound lags behind
two blue jet aeroplanes
        slipping so low, so fast
across the vast blue blue sky.

*

A shooting star, a fox,
clear night sky, light of the waning moon.

Up late talking: spiritual matters,
mind matters.

*

Friday night Throwleigh church bells
ring out from up the hill,
half an hour's walk away.

The sound carries down the valleys,
down to this Frog Mill, full of joy, full of the sound
of these church bells.

Jesus, Buddha: realized beings still speaking,
sounding out for centuries, millennia old now.
Talking about *sangha*, fellowship.

Now, look how we go through this old world,
not listening,
save for when somebody else, from somewhere,
comes along and says this: "Shut up. Listen."

DRINKING WINE WITH WESTRAY AFTER NOT SEEING HIM FOR A LONG TIME

Just one bottle tonight;
just a bit drunk and nothing,
nothing like the old days.

Now, people come, people go.
I see Westray, I don't.
Seeing people is always good
and after a bottle of wine
we can say goodbye casually
at midnight.

CREME EGG

Creme Egg.
Creme Egg.
Chocolate shell.
Weird thick cream.
What the hell?
Not exactly
what I'd dream
for the inside of an egg.

MISSION BURRITO

I buy for you, my love,
a burrito
(in the end, we are
like burritos: full of beans,
wrapped together).
Another burrito I buy for me
for one isn't enough for two
and though my love
of burritos is less than my love for you,
stay away from my burrito!
That's why I bought two.

THURSDAY NIGHT

Hung kuen kung fu
Chelsea Park *kouksundo*
Haedong kumdo
Tai chi   sit
Bike ride

In the Chelsea for a pint
with a geezer. San Miguel.

Crescent moon shining down soft.
      Moon lights the way.

IN THE DESERT WITH JESUS

How long to get over the hunger?
How long for the heat?
	Burning sun, cool to cold desert nights?
Did you feel lost?
And, when you discovered of your Father
that he was the same as you, did you rejoice,
dance, sing, pray, or simply walk back
to get something to eat?

IT NEVER LEAVES ME

That day,
Indian train ride
leaving out of Mumbai,
we lock eyes. A soundless connection,
me and this guy, eye to eye.
He's squatting on the tracks, lungi up.
My eyes shift towards the movement: shit,
like soft-serve chocolate ice cream,
coming out of his ass.

ON THE TV AT CASA CURVO

Bullfight!
Un hombre in pink socks
waves a red cape.

The bull – *El Toro*,
Taurus: I am the bull.
This bull, five spears in his left shoulder,
he breathes
heavy.

(Picture in picture: a man wheeled into an ambulance.)

I think *El Toro*, he is *muy furioso* with his balls and cock
heaving in time with his breath.

He rages at the cape.
He's nearly as tall as the man
       in the pink socks
who must have some fear, surely,
but turns his back to the bull.
Foam is flecked on the bull's hide.

Let me tell you something: I want that bull
to kick the man's ass, shove that rack of horns right up that pink-
       sock-wearing, tight-trousers-wearing dandy.

Coward. Put down your cape, your sword.
If only you had balls as big as that bull.
You stick your sword between the heaving
shoulder blades.

El Toro!
El Toro!
Ahora, muerto.
Four horses drag you
through the dust.

HOW I CAUGHT A FALLING BOTTLE

I caught that
falling bottle:
right hand reflex
across the body
palm reversed
and on my left.
Still deft I am, still quick.

LITTLE BABY JEREMY

*Little Baby Jeremy,
eighteen months in,
first life over.*

*Memory hides Illinois life: Little Baby Jeremy
don't remember nothing. Must've been so blue.*

*Where's Mama at? What to do?
Grandma, Grandpa, where'd they go?*

Now I don't remember nothing.
Eating and sleeping I surely did do,
but it must've been a sad and lonely day or two.

Leaving Illinois' central plains flat land,
going to Kentucky's fertile fields,
growing up a Toombs in Guthrie.

Must've been lonely, for a little while,
sitting alone, the lonely child,
Baby Jeremy, lonely awhile.
Sometime, somewhere, back there
for sure must've been smiles, love
for Little Baby Jeremy, sometimes still a lonely child.

CHINA EXHIBIT, BRITISH MUSEUM

So many Buddhas:
statues
heads
reliefs
carvings
hands
sketches
castings
and us humans,
with all possibility present.
Breathe in.
Breathe out.
We are not yet turned to stone.

FREEDOM

"Freedom," he said.
My head rose up
in recognition of desire
to go through, "go beyond."
"Freedom," he said.
I heard it ring through.

This was said by a yogi in India. A magical man was he. Spiritual. He asked a group of us foreigners if we'd like to come to his yoga class. I said no and walked on down the road. He caught up with me, but really he just appeared beside me and asked me again. I found myself saying "yes," not against my will, but certainly not with any consideration by my conscious mind.

¿WHO KNOWS?

Who knows the way it goes
as the globe spins?
Conspiracies! Mysteries!
Who killed Kennedy?
Who Dr. King?
Did we land on the moon?
Why'd Lennon have to go so soon?
¿Who knows?
      ¿Who knows?
           ¿Who knows?

Who knows what my dad did in his youth?
Because he ain't talkin'!

Who knows
is God is or is God ain't?
Is this world just a faint assembly of shadows?
¿Who knows?

When I contemplate Zen koans
I feel as if nothing can be known:
hair on teeth
drink tea
clap hand
tree falls
silent bang.

What's this thing there everybody's talkin' about,
some kinda trip or something folks are going on
in their own heads?
There's too many people on meds these days.
Why don't they just drink whiskey?
¿Who knows?

Like Mammaw always said,
It's hard tellin', not knowin'.
¿Who knows?

www.ingramcontent.com/pod-product-compliance
Lightning Source LLC
Chambersburg PA
CBHW021000090426
42736CB00010B/1395